$5.00

Being UP in a DOWN WORLD

Being UP in a DOWN WORLD

by

James E. Kilgore

BEING UP IN A DOWN WORLD

Irvine, CA 92714

Library of Congress Catalog Card Number 76-53065
ISBN #0-89081-057-5

Printed in the United States of America

DEDICATION

For My Mother, Whose Teaching Lives
Because Her Living Teaches

ABOUT THE AUTHOR

Dr. James Kilgore is a marriage and family counselor in Atlanta, Georgia. He is the president of the Northside Counseling Center and the International Family Foundation. The first is an organization which offers private, professional help to couples and individuals in need. The second organization is one of global scope, involved in bringing together centers helping families with problems in various countries and training people with professional skills in the area of marriage and family counseling, as well as, group dynamics.

''Jim,'' as most of his friends and clients know him, is married and has three teen-age children. A native Georgian, he has been educated and has lived in several sections of the United States, including the Southeast, California and Minnesota. He has earned degrees in the humanities, education and counseling. Prior to becoming a marriage and family counselor, he spent 15 years as a clergyman.

He is a fellow and approved supervisor of the American Association of Marriage and Family Counselors, Inc. He is also a certified sex therapist in the American Association of Sex Educators, Counselors and Therapists. His other professional memberships and certifications are listed in a number of national and international recognitions such as *Who's Who In The West, Who's Who in Georgia, Who's Who In The South and Southwest, The International Dictionary of Biography* and *Who's Who in Religion.*

He is the author of four other books: *Billy the*

Preacher, Pastoral Care of the Hospitalized Child, Being A Man In A Woman's World and *Getting More Family Out Of Your Dollar*. He has appeared on many radio and television programs including AM Los Angeles and Today in Georgia.

His offices are located at 204 Northside Medical Center, 275 Carpenter Drive, Atlanta, Georgia 30328.

PREFACE

Depression is the number one mental health symptom in our world today. Surveys indicate that as high as sixty percent of the people are unhappy *most* of the time! Ours is a *down* world personally for many people who, judging by their economic or social standing should "have it made."

If you have not yet experienced depression, you will probably have your chance in the future! Feeling down is a common problem. But the problems push for solutions. That's often where I come into contact with many people. For some, I am a professional counselor who listens to their problems; others share their "down" moments much more subtly—over coffee in a break at a conference, with a carefully worded question, or an almost offhand remark.

Dealing with depressed, disturbed, and lonely people does not insulate me from the same symptoms. I have been *down* too. From the process of dealing with others and coping with my own times of discouragement, I have gained some insights about getting *up* and staying there regularly.

This book is a basic approach to positive mental balance—a direction out of despair, a way *up* when you are down. I offer it in that spirit.

James E. Kilgore
Atlanta, Georgia

TABLE OF CONTENTS

PART ONE: PERSONAL GROWTH
"Growing All Your Life!"

PART TWO: PERSONAL PROBLEMS
"Coping With the Conflicts of Living"

PART THREE: PERSONAL COMMITMENT
"Tapping the Continuing Resources of Life"

PART FOUR: PERSONAL EXPERIENCE

"Integrating Your Insights Daily"

PART ONE
Personal Growth

"Growing All Your Life!"

"He who is not busy being born is busy dying."
—Bob Dylan

1

Introduction

"Life is like an onion; You peel off one layer at a time,
And sometimes you weep."
—Carl Sandburg

Welcome to the world of "upmanship"! But be warned of one thing. Self-exploration is like eating one potato chip. If you start, it is likely that you cannot quit. This is the bridge of no return. Risk the adventure at the peril of losing the safety of your naivete in simplicity. To grow emotionally is at times a happy experience; at other times not.

The group gathered for their first meeting. As they sat around the table, their faces betrayed the nervousness each felt. The leader entered and the session began. He talked positively and warmly about the purpose the group shared—to grow as persons. As he shared his own needs, it became easy for others in the group to share themselves with each other. A sense of belonging and acceptance started to develop.

Ten weeks later these same people who were fearful of each other on the first meeting found it difficult to leave. They paused to embrace each other and to express strong feelings of caring. Something had changed them! It was the experience of sharing, sensing, listening, and learning about themselves.

You can develop and use a formula that creates a growing sense of personhood and allows you to live a more satisfying life. In these pages you will find guidelines for staying *alive* all your life and enjoying the process of growing. And this emotionally vibrant life can be described by seven attributes:

Awareness
Articulation
Action
Actualization
Assessment
Affirmation
Achievement

Perceived, explored, and mastered, these concepts will help you achieve more fulfillment in each day's life.

In the following chapters you will be invited to explore yourself and to know yourself perhaps more deeply than you have ever explored or known before. It's the way to be up in a down world. Bon voyage!

2

Awareness

"The greatest gift one can give to another person is a deeper understanding of life and the ability to love and believe in Self."

—Chantal

The experience of becoming more aware of the various facets of *ME* is as mysteriously rewarding and as curiosity provoking as the experience of being blind and suddenly receiving sight. Interestingly, we can describe a form of awareness as insight. I sometimes "slip" and say, "in-light" in order to call attention to the spontaneous and somewhat surprising nature if insight. Almost as though a lamp has been turned on in a dark room, fresh ideas about ourselves can be seen "for the first time." Or we experience ourselves, hearing the same words, but sensing new meaning in those old phrases. One of the greatest teachers said to his listeners, "He who has ears to hear, let him hear."

THROUGH THE LOOKING GLASS

Insight is the ability to focus on and absorb ideas and reflections about ourselves which come to us from the mirrors of life. These mirrors may be basically intellectual in form such as the formal educational experience, reading books. listening to lectures, watching educational TV, and so forth. Or these mirrors may take the shape of other human beings who by their behavior provide reflections for us of our own mistakes or beneficent actions. As we absorb these reflections about ourselves from life, we learn more about ourselves. This process is called insight.

Insight is one of the primary goals of counseling. Whatever the training of the therapist—whether a psychiatrist, psychologist, social worker, marriage and family counselor, or a pastoral counselor—he will be concerned about helping the other person gain some kind of insight. Only those who specialize in behavior modification are likely to place less emphasis on the use of some form of insight in the therapy process.

The quest for insight is even stronger in personal growth groups. Here the group leader believes that life experiences provide in themselves a unique form of insight. In the normal and specialized encounters provided by the group setting, a person may learn more about himself and about others through observation, interchange, and education.

ORGANIZING MY INSIGHTS

But awareness is more than insight. It is also the processing of these insights into a more cohesive picture of oneself through which patterns of behavior emerge. One may be aware momentarily of a specific feeling or may be aware of a particular idea within the context of the single experience. However, the kind of awareness which we are concerned with here is the centralizing or "wholizing" awareness in which descriptions of myself begin to take significant shape. I begin to see myself in some organized conceptual way that "makes sense" against the backdrop of my life experiences. I may not like all these perceptions, or I may be overjoyed with them. But awareness is the process and not the feelings that I have about that process.

Awareness is the knowledge of myself and the willingness within my own mind to formulate that knowledge into organized groups.

Awareness is that inner expression with which I am comfortable or uncomfortable, but which I recognize within myself as reality. I may often be aware of parts of my personality or actions within my life which I find difficult to admit to others, but they do not escape me where I confront myself in the inner person.

Awareness is that deep room within the caverns of my being where I, like the witch in Snow White, come to the looking glass on the wall of my self-organization and say, "Mirror, mirror on the wall, what am I really like at all?"

3

Articulation

"How do I know what I am thinking until I see what I've said?"

—Sam Jones

A wonderful but strange relationship exists between self-knowledge and self-expression. Sidney Jourard says that understanding comes through expressing. My "transparency"—the ability to let another see through me—becomes the key to myself.[1]

What begins deep within me soon takes the form of words. Language is an essential form of communication. Speaking, in a sense, is giving life to my ideas. But this is not a new concept. The writer of the Hebrew story of creation (Genesis 1) says that God spoke the world into existence and blessed his work with the word, "good." In the New Testament, the word of God is revealed in flesh through the person of Jesus Christ.

WORDS DON'T COME EASILY

Therefore, the growing person adds to his awareness the dimension of articulation. But it is not easy. Some feelings and ideas within us seem inexpressible. We struggle for words that are adequate to convey our mental and emotional images.

On occasions I rehearse my words within but squelch their expression by my decision that your response will be judgmental. I fear sounding "stupid" or seeming "irrelevant" when I speak to you. My fears justify my hiding these feelings and remaining inexpressive.

You must then assume that you know my feelings or attempt to draw me out from my fearful shell. If you attempt to lead me to share my feelings, you may become vulnerable to the accusation of being nosey. There is safety and control in remaining silent. But loneliness is also present. I am isolated from you because I cannot or will not express my feelings openly. I may identify with you or feel that you are speaking my feelings too, but you cannot know that unless I speak to you.

When you respond with a message that I am heard by you, I sense new hope for this process of growth. Learning to articulate my feelings is a behavioral skill. The more I practice, the better I become. The more I share with you, the more you know me and the less isolated I am in my world.

FIVE FUNCTIONAL STEPS

Here are some important ways to help you articulate more clearly:

1. *Accept* the responsibility for your own feelings, thoughts, words and actions. Blaming another for what is yours creates barriers to communication, not bridges. When you "unload your responsibility," the burden will be felt but the message contained in it will usually be lost.

2. *Admit* your fears and anxieties about your ability to communicate. People identify more with your weaknesses than with your strengths. When you are uncomfortable, sharing that feeling evokes support. Pretending comfort emotes phoniness and distance to others.

3. *Concentrate* on the conversations of others. Give them your emotional commitment and your ears. Two results may surprise you: Not only will you hear them more clearly, but you will also hear yourself when you speak. Furthermore, you will find that since you are a good listener, people will hear you more carefully when you speak. The words that you hear from others, that is, their style, vocabulary and method of presentation will prove to be stimulants to you to change your own capabilities for revealing yourself.

4. *Reflect* what others say to you before you respond to them. If you have not heard them right, you can correct the error quickly. If you have received the message, that fact alone will precede

your thoughts beneficially. The atmosphere of your listening will provide stimulus for better attempts at sharing your feelings.

5. *Choose* the simplest and most direct way to express your feelings. When you have spoken, wait for a response before adding new data. Treat silence as a friend. Flailing the air with words is not communicating; it is simply making noise. Repeat what you've said only to clarify and then see if you can discover another way to express that idea or feeling if you must repeat it. Re-statement of an idea is redundant at best and boring at worst.

When you are aware of yourself and can articulate that knowledge, you have taken the first two steps in personal growth.

4

Action

"Strive always to be like a good watch: open-faced, busy hands, pure gold, well regulated, full of good works."

Words express my feelings; actions change my behavior. To express myself is hopeful, but to act on my intention is a positive movement toward change. My actions convey more than my words alone; movement reinforces meaning.

Verbally I profess; actively I fulfill. There is no assurance like action. As Justice Oliver Wendell Holmes, Jr. said, "I think that, as life is action and passion, it is required of a man that he should share the passion and action of his time, at peril of being judged not to have lived."[2]

Action converts passivity into motion. Belief without active demonstration is lifeless. To profess without production is depression. Action is the first step of commitment. It is the match that lights the candle against darkness. It is not the end; it is a beginning.

I ACT TO CHANGE THINGS

Action expresses my awareness and confirms my articulation. It is the hope for a new pattern in my living. Let me illustrate. Mark knew that his feelings about Sharon were changing. What had once been a roaring forest fire of love in his heart had dwindled to a flickering ember in just three years. He knew something was wrong. One day he admitted to a friend that he was troubled about his marriage. But at that time he did nothing more about it.

Sharon was depressed. She too felt like she was "losing Mark" because her feelings of love were waning. They were drifting apart. She confided her feelings of discomfort to a neighbor. She wanted to seek professional help, but her fear of Mark's reactions caused her to procrastinate.

By a coincidence of scheduling each of them phoned my office on referrals from their friends and made appointments to see me for marriage counseling. Can you imagine their surprise when each came home that evening feeling prepared to reveal their big step to the other? Each took action, and the courage gained from that step brought change in their relationship. Making that initial appointment was an explosion that broke the log jam in their lives and began a fresh start "downstream."

A decision to do something brings relief. Acting on the decision builds confidence in myself, and enhances future change possibilities.

START TODAY

The challenge to action has been caught so beautifully in these words;

Trust no future, how e're pleasant!
Let the dead past bury its dead;
Act, act in the living present;
Heart within, and God o'er head;

Lives of great men all remind us
We can make our lives sublime,
And, departing, leave behind us
Footprints on the sands of time.
A Psalm of Life
by Henry W. Longfellow

Today is the first day of the rest of your life; act like it!

5

Actualization

"Every man's foremost task is the actualization of his unique, unprecedented and never recurring potentialities, and not the repetition of something that another . . .even the greatest, has already achieved."
—*Martin Buber*

Actualization is a word associated with the human potential movement in psychology. People like Abraham Maslow, Virginia Satir, and Everett Shostrom have added greater meaning to the word. Personal growth moves on the ability to become whole. Growing people are engaged in a process of continual change—that flow of change is called actualization.

Action is the beginning point—the first step of movement from which change springs. Actualization is the continuing struggle to walk in the direction I've begun. An actualizer is willing to act regularly on what he *has* learned and *is* learning about himself. In his own outreach for interaction the actualizer invites others to share the process and to become whole themselves. My actualizing behavior gives birth to my own freedom and models the role of liberation life for you.

LIBERTY IS A STYLE OF LIFE

Nationally, we proclaim our right to "life, liberty, and the pursuit of happiness." In our efforts to interact with other nations, we hold to the faith that our republic will exemplify democracy for them. We fight to defend our own freedom and sometimes the freedom of others. Ideally, by our actions we create an atmosphere in which that liberty will thrive.

Personally, to live the actualizing life is to struggle for your own freedom and to create an atmosphere which invites others to reach for more of their own personal potential.

Mary Anne was bitterly depressed when I met her. Most of her energy was being used to attack her husband because of his inadequacies as a man. She blamed him for the "trap" of her life. It was his fault her needs were not being met. She was sure that she *deserved* a divorce but feared that as an answer to her problem.

I often see people who are caught in the same conflict. Blaming others for my feelings is one way of avoiding my own responsibility.

Initially, I supported Mary Anne's plan for a divorce, but as we worked together, I used each opportunity to remind her of the role in her life that Roger played—he was her emotional "whipping boy." "Who will you blame when he is no longer in your life?" I asked.

Months passed as she took the journey into self-awareness. First, she began to articulate her feelings clearly. Then came her first action steps. Working in a personal growth group, she continued in the pattern of insight. Her depression disappeared. She identified some of its causes and began coping with her own life responsibilities.

As Mary Anne changed, Roger could not continue his old patterns. At first he became angry; then he was depressed. He adopted Mary Anne's "old" symptoms and finally, he came into therapy. Their renewed and exciting marriage now is the direct result of her actualizing behavior. She faced her own conflict and allowed Roger to accept his own problems. Together they spurred each other on in their growth. Their marriage is now a positive competition for personal growth. Each of them is enjoying greater freedom and happiness.

WITHOUT YOU THE WORLD IS LESS

Actualization is the commitment to continue in your personal pursuit of wholeness. Inherent within your journey is the freedom for others to share the pilgrimage. Since your potential is unique, only you can give the world your particular combination of skills, feelings, and interaction. Your enriched life means the stimulation of nerve endings which might otherwise never be exercised. Without you, all of "us" may not discover some parts of ourselves. The spark of your life now may produce a fire to keep you warm against the cold loneliness of a winter of discontent in the future.

Actualize; don't fossilize!

6

Assessment

"God grant me the serenity to accept the things I cannot change, the courage to change the things I can, and the wisdom to know the difference."

Evaluation of progress in our growth is essential to the process. I've always been amused at the words of Sam Jones, the philosopher: "How do I know what I'm thinking until I see what I've said?"

A TEST OF MATURITY

Assessing my growth honestly and accurately is one of the tests of maturity. But the stages of growth become increasingly difficult even as they become more rewarding. Chronology can be measured in days, months, and years. Personal growth is evaluated in three different modes; self-satisfaction, responses from others, and situational progress toward appropriate goals.

Each individual can develop his own "self-satisfaction scale" for life. Against those measures he can judge his progress. In my 40 years I have come to rely on five ingredients to assess my satisfaction in life—integrity, challenge, theory, understanding, and sensitivity.

Integrity means for me a sense of consistent self-revelation. I assess that by asking myself the question, "Am I being true to what I know of myself now?" To assess life's challenge for me, I ask, "Am I still eager to pursue the goals I have set for myself?" When I check out my direction in life, I ask, "Do I know where I am going?" The theory of my life is the balance between the direction I am moving and whether or not it makes "sense" to me. To assess understanding, I ask, "Do I comprehend and integrate regularly the ideas and events of my existence?" For sensitivity, "Does my life have room for the needs of people important to me and time for personal responses to them?"

I cannot be satisfied with my life if there is not substantial progress within this functional framework. My personal "success" is measured in these terms. I am the final judge of my behavior's satisfaction.

FEEDBACK TEACHES ME

A part of my assessment data, however, is the responses I get from other people. In personal growth groups we commonly refer to this process as "feedback." What comes back to me from you becomes input for my assessment.

I have learned some lessons about feedback which particularly guide me in groups. Let me share them with you.

Good feedback is not an opinion. When people say to me, "I think this about you," my first inclination is to accept what they have said but to label it as "opinion." If your opinion and my opinion differ, I will almost always be able to discredit your opinion. If have low self-esteem, I will disregard the positive aspects of your opinion. If I am defensive, I will minimize the critical part of your statements.

Good feedback is not analysis. When I interpret the behavior of others, I threaten them emotionally. To say to you what your thoughts or actions mean is to assume that I know more about you than you do. When I analyze your past, you may be impressed with my knowledge; but you will exercise care in future conversations lest I hear something you did not realize you were saying.

Good feedback is a report of your feelings, experiences, observations, or senses. To respond effectively to others, I describe how I experience them. Some good ways to do this are by saying, "What I feel is . . ." or "I heard this when you talked . . ." Another good guideline is to use your senses directly, such as "I see," "I hear," or "I experience you as . . ." The more specific and direct my responses to you, the less likely you are to be confused.

As I assess my personal growth in personal dimensions, your response to me helps me see, feel, and hear myself through your eyes. Your feedback becomes my "mirror" in which I can discover reflections of myself. Without feedback I experience difficulty in knowing more fully the "blindsides" in my life. Yet you see that aspect more clearly and can open my eyes by your reports.

HOW FAR HAVE I COME?

The third dimension of my assessment is the progress I make toward goals I have set for myself. A later chapter deals with goal setting, but let me mention the standards for evaluation here. There are three significant questions I use in gauging my movement toward a goal. First, what have I actually done to accomplish the results I wanted? Too often I want things that I must depend on others to obtain for me or that they must do on my behalf. My level of pleasure may well be proportionate to my own effort to accomplish my goals.

Second, in the light of what I now know, is the goal I set for myself realistically obtainable? If the goal is unrealistic, then it is appropriate for me to re-evaluate my commitment and direction.

Third, what does the accomplishment I have presently obtained teach me for future goal-setting?

Evaluation, or assessment, reveals where I am in life

and points me in the directions I want to continue. I am not ending my journey; I am checking the road map to note my progress and the directions I'll travel later.

7

Affirmation

"A friend is one who knows you as you are, understands where you have been, accepts who you have become and still invites you to grow."

Attitude restructuring is built on the backbone of affirmation. To affirm change in myself is a great step of assurance.

In transactional analysis affirmation is the confirmation of new data in the ego state. It is by assessment, replacement and affirmation that "updating" occurs. Look at this illustration.

NEW DATA EQUALS NEW BEHAVIOR

Joan was born into a family where she learned to be "the black sheep." She got negative feedback so regularly that she depended on hearing it. When I first met her and said some positive things to her, she accused me of lying to manipulate her. Since my response to her was what I honestly felt and saw, I repeated her feedback. Over several hours of talking together, she acknowledged that she wanted to believe these "good" ideas about herself. Reassuring her, I continued to feed new data into her experiential "computer." When she joined a group, she reverted to the old patterns. I was disappointed for her, but the group did not reinforce her negative images. In time she began to adjust her thinking and to feel differently. I will remember for a long time the day Joan exclaimed, "I am OK! I don't have to apologize for being me!" The tears flowed from her eyes and a new confidence was born within her. As she has affirmed positive mental attitudes, change has occurred. Conflicting ideas are still a part of her experience, but by continuing affirmation the "new" Joan keeps growing and the "old" Joan is diminishing in strength.

AFFIRMATION BY REPETITION

Maintenance of behavior is an affirmation, however subtle it may seem. If you continue to behave in a specific manner, you are in reality choosing to act that way. We change what we really dislike about ourselves. If we cannot do it alone, then we ask for help. What we live is what we really believe.

Gifts from friends mean a great deal to me. A large rock, sliced in half and polished smoothly in the center, sits on the book shelf in my office. In the "cut" side of the rock are carved the words, "If you don't live it, you don't believe it." Bill gave me the engraved rock to remind me of an experience in a group when I said those words to him.

He was a busy man full of projects and enjoying success within his company. He came to our group because he wanted to learn how to relate to people so that he could be more effective in managing his time. He professed love for his wife and children. Often he said, "They come first in my life." One night I grew tired of his verbage and simply confronted him with the statement: "If you don't *live* it, you don't *believe* it." For Bill that feedback became a turning point in his life. The rock is our mutual memory stimulant of that meaningful moment.

If you continue to behave in certain patterns, that becomes your life "confession of faith." I *affirm* my beliefs by my actions. I believe only what I live.

EXPERIENCE CANNOT BE DENIED

If we are different, our affirmation is "I have changed and I like my new experience or behavior." The force of such affirmation is caught in that New Testament story of the healing of the blind man (John 9). When asked how it happened, he described the events. Pressed further by his accusers as to the righteousness of his healer, the man responded with this positive declaration; "I only know this: I was blind, but now I can see."

Insight is having our eyes opened to ourselves. When

I act on that awareness, new behavior produces new results. Assessing those results, I affirm those parts I enjoy and discard what I no longer wish to pursue in my life-style. What I affirm continues to be a part of me, even if it is only affirmed in my behavior.

To be a friend to myself is to know where I have been and where I am going and to encourage my right and my pursuit of the journey.

8

Achievement

"Lord, when we are wrong, make us willing to change, and when we are right, make us easy to live with."
—Peter Marshall

The final stage of the seven steps to personal growth is measured change. Affirmation is my decision and acknowledgement that I like where I am going in life; achievement is the continuing advancement in that direction.

Integrating the changes I have affirmed into new patterns of my behavior is the capstone of my growth. One of the marks of that kind of maturity is a consistency born out of self-discipline.

DISCIPLINE ADVANCES

Disciplined living flows from personal commitment. Lack of discipline is often seen as impulsiveness, which is born out of boredom and transient appeal. The frenetic and changeable patterns that result create anxiety and insecurity. Compulsiveness, which is another form of the lack of discipline, also holds little personal reward. It is born out of a necessity to please others. I fear failing to live up to the expectations I sense; thus I drive myself toward perfectionistic aims. I am doomed to fail in some way. Nothing I do will ever be "good enough." I will *always* fall just short of what I could have done. It is impossible for me to please every person in my life and to meet all their expectations. Compulsiveness arises out of that misdirected hope that I can please everyone.

On the other hand, discipline is the freedom to fulfill my responsibilities well and to be able to make choices as to how I do that. Every commitment I make creates some limits on my freedom as well as restricting my responsibilities. The mature man moves ahead in life by the strength of his commitments. He *lives* to sense, speak, act, share, evaluate, affirm and grow. Life is not his destination; it is his daily journey. Happiness is in the pleasures of each day, not the rewards of some future event.

These seven steps provide a backdrop for living the "upmanship" life and for coping with our daily problems. The maturity which results contributes to maintaining the characteristics of the "up" life. You can be *up* in a down world. Try it; you'll like it!

PART TWO
Personal Problems

"Coping With the Conflicts of Living"

"Fear knocked at the door. Faith answered.
No one was there."
—Author Unknown

9

Depression

"You pray in your distress and in your need; would that you might pray also in the fulness of your joy and in your days of abundance."

—*Kahlil Gibran*

Depression is the most frequently used word to describe emotional symptoms. Most of us are depressed at some time in our lives. Some do not recognize the symptoms. They drag through each day, not knowing that life can be different. What they experience as "normal" may be depression.

To be depressed is to function at a low level of emotional interaction—to be blocked from within oneself. Since this is a complex phenomena, it may appear in different symptoms with passive, defensive, aggressive or other overtones. At the simplest level depression is the experience of life as "down." When I feel drained of energy, apathetic and just "can't get excited about anything," I am probably depressed.

FIVE CONTRIBUTING CAUSES

There are five basic causes of depression which have clearly emerged in the people I've known in professional counseling. The factors contributing to depression are:

1. Chemical or biological imbalance
2. Unresolved guilt
3. Unexpressed anger
4. Fear of failure
5. A sense of isolation

Let's examine them more closely.

CHEMICAL OR BIOLOGICAL IMBALANCE

In my experience, less than 10 percent of the cases of depression I encounter are of a physical origin. What is called "post partum depression," the let down experience in the first few months after the birth of a child, is common among younger females. A few cases related to levels of blood sugar or dietary imbalance are also seen. The great majority of those I have referred to medical doctors for a checkup receive negative reports. Yet most cases of depression are treated by chemotherapy, or medication. A good physician will acknowledge that this is only a stop gap treatment of the symptoms, while ignoring the cause. My own clinical knowledge says that you cannot touch the emotional cause of depression with a chemical solution. Let's look further, then, at the kinds of non-chemical "downs" we experience.

UNRESOLVED GUILT

Guilt takes a heavy toll on emotional energy. Hobart Mowrer suggested in his writings that "Confession to others is an appropriate way of treating depression."[3] This is based on his observation that a good deal of depression is caused by guilt. Relieving my guilt frees my emotional resources for other uses. A good place to uncover the cause of your "down" feelings is to examine your relationships. Have I wronged someone? Can I identify a relationship about which I feel guilty? Admitting those feelings resolves much of the depression.

Rational, or real guilt, is different from irrational, or neurotic, guilt. The real thing, known or rational guilt, can be dealt with through action. I can make restitution in some form—an apology, a re-payment or a substitutionary action. Verbal offenses can be made right verbally. Physical offenses with physical actions. There is a balancing action for the cause of my guilt.

On the other hand, neurotic, or irrational guilt is usually unknown to anyone but me. I alone must deal with my guilt. Much of this neurosis is based on my inability to live up to the expectations I assume others have of me. Some of my guilt may result from my own unrealistic demands on myself. When I recognize that I cannot be perfect, I begin to resolve this guilt. It is this neurotic feeling that is best addressed in Fritz Perls' now famous lines:

"I do my thing and you do your thing.
I am not in this world to live up to your expectations,
And you're not in this world to live up to mine.
You are you and I am I,
And if by chance we find each other,
It's beautiful."

UNEXPRESSED ANGER

Anger hidden within us is another major cause of depression. These feelings may create some physical symptoms such as an ulcerated stomach or intestinal disturbances. People plagued with guilt frequently suffer headaches and neck pains. These unexpressed feelings do damage to us—not only internally, but they also can create destructiveness in our relationships. Hidden anger has a way of erupting when we least expect it to and often at a most inopportune moment.

How often our anger toward a spouse is vented on a child! The angry frustration of the job depressed us, but our family members are hurt by its release. Hurt and anger are opposite poles of a continuum. At one end is anger and at the other end is hurt. Often when I feel hurt, I get angry and retaliate. Sometimes when I'm angry and do not express it, I get hurt and weak. I need to express both feelings. Unexpressed anger is like a sponge; it absorbs my energy and I begin to feel depressed.

FEAR OF FAILURE

When I feel like I am going to fail, I sometimes react with passivity. This "trapped" or situational depression is frequent among males.

A 46-year-old man came for counseling on referral from his physician. He was depressed and had begun to lose his sexual drive. As we talked about his symptoms, I discovered that he was the vice-president of a family owned business. While he made a good salary, he was only two years younger than the president of that firm. He had peaked out vocationally, but he was unable to express his feeling of being trapped. He needed the security of his present salary, but he felt no challenge for the future. He was depressed because he had 19 years of boredom ahead of him.

The same kind of feelings are present when a couple feels locked into a marriage "going nowhere." Teenagers experience this depression when they feel that their family members are just putting up with each other because "they have to do it." When I face a situation in which I feel trapped or a problem I *can't* overcome, a profound sense of heaviness drags me "down." I am depressed.

A SENSE OF ISOLATION

The fifth contributor to depression is a feeling of being alone. "Feeling cut off" is a description I hear often.

A 62-year-old woman was depressed. Her husband had died five years earlier; and since he was gone, she had become less and less active. She spent a week or more at a time in her apartment seeing no one but her cat. She was isolated! Her depression had a real cause. She began to feel better simply because she got dressed up and came to my office. She had no serious mental problem, but her "homework" became the therapy of active involvement. As she re-entered her world and engaged people in relationships, her "down" feelings vanished.

Feeling isolated within yourself—that sense of being "lonely in a crowd"—is dealt with much like the widow in her world. Break out of your shell and make contact with another person.

THE "UP" LIFE

The person who learns to be "up" in a down world faces depression realistically. The five obvious steps for dealing with your negative feelings are:

1. Get a physical checkup to rule out chemical imbalance. Or if you have been under a heavy schedule, take some time off and rest. Restore your body with a holiday. A weak body is more susceptible to depression.

2. Acknowledge your guilt to the appropriate person or people. Confess your wrongdoing; make restitution in any way you can. A sense of cleansing is a great aphrodisiac to the spirit.

3. Express your anger. Psychologically the open admission of angry feelings "burns" a path toward another person. He can cross it in a response to

you. You will probably be amazed to find a ready response to your feelings. When we express our feelings, we very often discover that they are not nearly as big and awesome as they seemed when they were hidden within us.

4. Risk failure by doing something. Break out of your trap. Don't just sit there; do something. Look for another job, talk to your family about your fears. There is always the chance that someone sees life differently and will tell you so.

5. Reach out of your loneliness to another person. Every human being has some feelings of isolation within. If you plug into that arena in another person, a lifetime friendship may be born.

Coping with depression is possible, but there are other problems as well. Let's move on.

10

Anxiety

A prayer to be said when the world has gotten you down, and you feel rotten, and you're too doggone tired to pray, and you're in a big hurry and besides you're mad at everybody . . . . .HELP!

—Author Unknown

In addition to being depressed, many people are anxious. They are seeking something, but they do not know what it is.

Soren Kierkegaard defined anxiety as "the alarming possibility of being able." It is the middle area between potential success and possible failure. Anxiety is like a responsibility: if I fulfill it well, good feelings emerge; if I fail, my feelings are negative. As with depression, the symptoms of anxiety are varied: sweaty palms, rapid breathing, tension of body muscles and other manifestations. Defining anxiety is difficult because it is an unspecified sense of foreboding. In contrast to a specific fear, anxiety is a generalized fear. I fear one man pointing a gun at my face. But anxiety is like feeling that somewhere, ten different men are pointing rifles at my back.

While anxiety is related to fear, there are other causes. The momentary feeling of "butterflies" in the stomach before going on stage or rising to address a large group is normal. When the feelings persist and paralyze me from action, my anxiety becomes serious. Most of us experience anxiety at some time.

Good performers in drama learn to cope with "stage fright" which is a form of anxiety. More relevant to many of us is what has been called the "television tremor," the feeling experienced just before you go on camera or when the radio talk show host introduces you. After the appearance is under way, comfort begins to return.

When these situational feelings pervade my everyday living, anxiety can become a destructive force in my existence.

ESTRANGEMENT

Like depression, anxiety occurs from feeling alone or isolated. Thomas Wolfe describes it this way:

> *"Naked and alone we come into exile. In her dark womb, we did not know our mother's face, from the prison of her flesh have we come into the*

unspeakable and incommunicable prison of this world. Which of us has known his brother? Which of us has looked into his father's heart? Which of us has not remained prisonpent? Which of us is not forever a stranger and alone."

—Thomas Wolfe, Look Homeward Angel

The feeling of being out of place or unattached is caught in this section of a poem by W. H. Audin.

This stupid world where
Gadgets are gods and we go on talking
Much about much, but remain alone
Alive but alone, belonging—where?
Unattached as a tumbleweed.

—W. H. Audin, The Age of Anxiety

Estrangement gives rise to our fears of others. The anxiety may persist in human behavior until it becomes manifest in a deeper trauma such as paranoia (extreme suspicion and fear).

Another contribution to anxiety is a sense of meaninglessness—the feeling that I have no purpose. This anxiety may actually reflect a feeling of being "cut off" from myself. These people speak of "not knowing myself."

LOSS OF PURPOSE

A businessman, caught in the demands of his industry, recently confided to me that he felt like a robot. "Today I listen to my wife; later I'll obey my boss; when does the real Bob do what he wants?" That is the question of meaning—what is reality? I am anxious when I feel caught up in the flow of life without some control as though being in a boat without oars caught in the strong current of the river and wondering if the noise I hear ahead is a waterfall.

Meaninglessness gives rise to persistent anxiety. Pushed to its extreme, its symptoms are detachment, lack of response, or an emotionally comatose condition.

In order to get up when anxiety drags me down, I have to accept the control (or responsibility) of my feelings. A basic way to minimize feelings of estrangement and lack of purpose is to build new relationships. While this is no simple task, I can begin to engage other people by:

1. Attempting to express understanding and concern for others. In order to do this I must give up the preoccupation with my own anxiety to become aware of what others need.

2. Communicating what I feel and speaking as directly to people as I can. I must not get embroiled in topics unrelated to the experience between us. Feelings of belonging grow out of sharing with others.

3. Returning appreciation. When someone warms me with a gesture, I should acknowledge it and respond. Anxiety breeds on what I see as unimportant or unnoticed overtures between people. I need to be sensitive to my opportunities to affirm others through response to them.

Brooding on the feelings within me increases their importance and allows those problems to dominate my living. As I open myself to new feelings and ideas, my estrangement is minimized and life takes on new meaning and a more positive reflection of my self-worth.

Low self-worth is the third conflict with which we must cope and that's our next chapter.

11

Low Self-Esteem

"It's really a wonder that I haven't dropped all my ideals, because they seem so absurd and impossible to carry out. Yet I keep them because in spite of everything I still believe that most people are really good at heart."

—Anne Frank

The California Indians have a tragic saying, "In the beginning God gave everyone a cup from which to drink. Our cup is broken." It is almost impossible to drink from a broken cup. It is just as difficult to be *up* when your self-worth is *down*.

In traveling for a non-profit organization, The International Family Foundation,[4] I have visited numerous countries. I came back from an overpopulated nation burdened by what seemed to be a total lack of value placed on the individual human life by that society. These impressions came from situations that involved the value of physical life. And yet each day I meet someone here in my own country, where life is valued, who is questioning his worth, values or the meaning of his existence, both physical and emotional.

REFLECTIONS OF SELF-ESTEEM

One shows his self-esteem in many ways. His actions give a strong clue to his self-esteem. Virginia Satir has given us insight into self-esteem in her personality styles. The life positions she describes fall into five categories:

The *placator* type says to the rest of the world, "I am worthless—you're worthy!" He shows that he is not worth much to himself by putting everybody else first at the expense of his own feelings and value. Socially, he is extremely polite and is known as the "nice guy." Emotionally, this person takes the "spaghetti position" in life—he just lies there and takes anything that is heaped on top of him.

The *blamer* type says, "I'm worthy—you're worthless!" He attacks everyone, accusing them of being at fault. His social behavior is critical and he thinks he gains by devaluing others around him. He points accusing and blaming fingers at others.

The *calculator* type says, "I'm not worthy, but you're not worthy either." He believes that only situations count. He appeals to causes and circumstances for which both you and he should sacrifice yourselves.

The *distractor* type says "Nothing is worth anything!" He makes a great entertainer and socially may be the life of the party, but he never shares himself because he sees himself as worthless too.

The *actualizer* type says everything has worth and shows it by taking people, events, and himself seriously in the actions and feelings he shares. He may be in difficulty socially from time to time because of the risk involved in being honest with people, but he believes it is worth that kind of risk to openly take others seriously.[5]

Self-esteem is *reflected* in your actions.

REDEFINING ESTEEM

A more important measure of self-esteem for me is that part which I invest in others. Try these two concepts on for size: a man who believes in his own worth has more to offer the world around him, and everything you invest in others retains value for you. Self-esteem is self-worth or value. Investing myself in another is a gift of value. The more I value myself the more I have to give and also to gain. Value is a bestowed trait.

After supporting an orphan boy in Korea for several years, my wife and I visited his hometown and the orphanage where he lives. We have three children who are ours by birth, but this little man was very special. Why? Because we had invested ourselves in him.

Low self-esteem is basically a matter of no outreach in life. Here are three ideas to help you increase your self-worth.

1. Realistically assess your strength as an individual. Identify those areas you want to share with others and work to improve them. Minimize the dependence of others on your areas of weakness.

2. Determine at least three ways you can begin to "invest" yourself in others. Take one step at a time until you've done all three. Evaluate your efforts and progress.

3. Accept the efforts of those around you to share themselves with you. No man can be free to give fully until he is also free to receive fully.

The results will have you "up" on your own self-worth scale!

12

Loneliness

"He who endures with patience is a conqueror."

We have discussed loneliness as an aspect of both anxiety and depression, but its presence creates a special "down" feeling to be observed more closely. There is a sense in which life is a search for the end of loneliness. Maturity is the ability to function in the world independently. A child grows from a relatively great state of dependence into a state of independence. Maturing intrinsically demands that one stand alone at some of the crucial points in life. How he deals with loneliness is then a statement of one's level of maturity.

Philosophies of life are built on the ways we deal with our loneliness. The existentialist so totally accepts his loneliness that it robs him of life's meaning. The hedonist dissipates his loneliness in pleasure. The fearful and dependent man seeks ways to escape his loneliness in diversion, addictions of various sorts or through people on whom he can be dependent.

A TOUCH OF REALITY

Life is full of lonely experiences. Real descriptions help us get in touch with them best. Here is one produced by a counselee while she was absent from a group session.

> Loneliness is a motel room with an extra bed and no T.V.
>
> Loneliness is to be alone at a reunion where everyone else has a mate and their children.
>
> > Love is when a favorite aunt pulls you aside and says, "Tell me about Ted and the children!"
>
> Loneliness is watching the sunset behind the San Francisco Peaks in Arizona, knowing at that moment in space and time there's no other sunset exactly like it in the world, and having no one to share it with.
>
> > Love is an old Indian, "It's beautiful, no?"
>
> Loneliness is to have a stroke at 78, to sit at the breakfast table, pointing at eggs, and ask your wife, "What are these things?" only to be told, "John, you certainly know what they are; you've been eating them every morning for 25 years!"
>
> > Love is the strength to smile and say, "Eggs, Honey," for 25 more years if necessary.
>
> Loneliness is a weekend at home when your hus-

band and children are gone and the house groans with the emptiness.

> Love is the raucous "Meow" of our old Siamese cat telling me she still thinks I'm purr-fect.

Loneliness is sitting here watching the Pacific surf pounding in and thinking, "God, it is big!" There's a sense of aloneness even on a crowded beach, but it can be overwhelming when viewed by yourself.

> Love is sharing thoughts and emotions with someone.

Loneliness is a feeling of being left out of the mainstream of life. It's thinking you are somehow different and set apart—it's wondering whether all that's gone before was really uplifting or simply another of life's disappointments. Loneliness is a feeling that the world is indifferent. To be unable to love or show emotion is to be mentally bankrupt.

Today, I make this commitment:

> TO LOVE—for in giving love, I will be loved.
>
> I'll be there to say, "It's beautiful, no?"
>
> "Tell me about the wife and kids!"
>
> "Eggs, Honey" and
>
> "You're just purr-fect, all of you!"

DEATH: WHERE EACH STANDS ALONE

Death is the ultimate lonely experience. How I view

death may then be a clue to the ways I cope with life's lonely experiences.

For over 10 years I have been leading people in groups where we explore our resources and attempt to discover more effective ways to cope with life's problems. In the groups, we use an exercise dealing with death. Each member is assigned this situation in advance:

> You have a rare disease. It will kill you in exactly six weeks, although you will not experience any change in the capacity of your body until your last hour of life. No one will be able to tell that you are going to die. What are you going to do with your last six weeks of life?

Take time to do this exercise yourself; it will prove to be an enlightening experience.

I want to share with you one woman's response. It was written in the form of a letter to God. It speaks for itself.

> Dear God:
> I have just come from the doctor's office and the news that was given me was the same that other doctors gave me. I will die in six weeks. Me, the typical married housewife, married almost 19 years and with four children. Somehow I feel frightened and alone. What will become of my children?
>
> God, do you hear me, why are you doing this? My job on earth isn't finished. There is still so much that I should do and so much that I have been waiting for. But I always thought there was time. Now you are taking away all my dreams

and my hopes for a better tomorrow. Will you comfort me, God, in these next six weeks? Will you let me feel your presence?

You see, God, I feel I have failed you and myself. I didn't make very good use of these 40 years. Before I saw the doctors I had slowly come to the conclusion that I would have to divorce my husband. But now I don't have to worry about that, do I God? You are taking care of that tremendous problem for me. You are divorcing us. I'm sorry I wasn't a better wife but I have loved him, the father of my children, and a part of him still loves me. Thank you for making me a woman. It has been a fantastic and beautiful experience. Above all, thank you for children; they are magnificent. I remember the day I shook my fist at you when I heard the doctors say they had epilepsy. I did feel your presence then; you helped me to accept what was unacceptable. How proud I am now of those two children. I always felt you made these children who society calls exceptional children, very, very exceptional. Help them with their tomorrows, God, all four of them. Give them a place in the sun. Make them work for their happiness and always help them to be aware of others.

Today I reread that line in a poem that I gave my son many years ago. It means so much to me now. "The woods are lonely, dark and deep but I have promises to keep and miles to go before I sleep." You have given me six more weeks on this beautiful earth. Your timing was great.

Next week I will see my firstborn daughter graduate from high school. She is the one they told me only had borderline intelligence along with her epilepsy. But how come she speaks French with such a flair and writes so beautifully and was accepted to the college of her first choice?

But I worry about my son. I wish I had a little more time with him. He is such a radical. He's tried pot and that scares me. But he has such a love of life that I almost envy him. I think he'll be OK. He's been so sweet to me these past few months when we've been separated. He has told me I look pretty. He's invited me out to the movies because he knew no one else would.

My daughter is strong but she needs me; watch over her, God. I'm going to enjoy them these next six weeks. I'd like to take them to the ocean again and watch them in the salt water. I love the water and the sand and so do they. The rest of the time I'm going to stay right here and do what I've always done; the washing, the ironing, the shopping and the caring. I don't want a Paris dress or a cruise around the world. I just want to enjoy my tomorrows right here.

I'd like to see my mother, my stepfather and my sisters before I die. I have missed them since I've been in Georgia. And the father of my Shirley Temple days, you know, God, my dad.

> The one who left when I was only two, and I've hated and loved and missed him all these years. It was strange seeing him a month ago in that awful nursing home, a tired old man dying of alcoholism. Did he hear me when I told him that I love him? I know I've been a rotten Catholic, for that I ask your forgiveness and your mercy. I never forgot you though and I always loved and needed your love. And I did feel that you were always there.
>
> I don't know what to say about my husband. Only you know what's been in my heart these years. I did love him but I wasn't his girl, his only girl. And that was what I had to be. Take care of him. I'm not shaking my fist at you anymore, God. I'm glad I've lived. But would you do me one favor, God? Before I leave, would you send someone to me to love me even if it is only for six weeks?

To be loved and living and unafraid of dying is the secret of being *up* in a *down* world. In the next section of this book I want to share with you both how to be loved and how to be unafraid.

PART THREE

Personal Commitment

"Tapping the Continuing Resources of Life"

''Let us leave the surface and, without leaving the world, plunge into God.''

—Teilhard De Chardin

13

Putting Things Into Perspective

"Ye shall know the truth, and the truth shall make you free."

—John 8:32

Not long ago a fellow professional cornered me in a meeting of marriage and family counselors and said, "I'm going to find out your secret of success if I have to keep you up all night. What is it?" I was frankly a bit irritated at being detained from my sleep, but I decided to try to answer his question. Here's some of what I said.

"I am a successful man in human relationships. I listen to people, and you've asked me the wrong question. The secret to my accomplishments in life is in three relationships—my relationship to me, my relationship to others, and my relationship to God!" My colleague was surprised at what I said.

TRUTH IS NOT DIVIDED

Let me share with you three important insights that have helped me put things into the right perspective.

First, *truth* is the same in every arena of life. No conflict exists between psychological, philosophical, theological or sociological truth. Only my understanding of that truth is inconsistent. The errors exist in my perception or description, not in the nature of truth.

The second insight is that truth in its highest and best form is personal. Living truth—that expressed in action, passion and continuity—supercedes all pronouncements or theoretical statements.

The third lesson is that truth is best learned in relationships. In a relationship, life, love and truth combine.

If that sounds a bit philosophical, let me personalize it. From my early childhood I have wanted to be *somebody*. I was not born in a socially high class family or to wealthy parents; we were just average, middle-class folks. To complicate matters, I was a rather fat, obnoxious kid. However, when I was 15 years of age, a moment of decision about my life began a process which has continued to this very day. That experience has brought about dynamic changes and significant successes which I enjoy and cherish, but cannot fully explain. The process involves a day by day faith that God is interested in me and at work on my behalf in the experiences of my living. What has happened is that I have had a confidence that I am not alone in the world since a quiet moment when I invited Jesus Christ to be Lord of my life.

For the last 25 years I have been becoming somebody in a significant way. I recognize that I am a unique person whom God loves. Because God cares about me, I am free from my preoccupation with myself so that I may react responsively to the needs of others. I am also capable of accepting the care and concern of others for me. Love has taken on new meanings, both broad and specific.

FAITH IS LIVING

Religion is not the *answer* to life. My faith *is* living out an integration of the conceptual knowledge I have about God, myself and others. I am not "Christian" because I live a certain way; I live that way because I am a believer. My faith radiates from my life-style, my priorities, and my relationships.

Being born again means to be plugged in to a new power source, an energizer for fully human experiences. Without being stimulated and maintained by the spirit of Christ, life is crippled and maimed, even dead. With a living relationship I am alive to new peak experiences in relationships not only with God, but with others.

Let me illustrate. On Christmas day, my nine-month-old nephew died suddenly while my sister and her husband were visiting us. In a matter of moments our happy cheer was transformed into deep sorrow. Two days later we were preparing for the funeral. Johnny, the five-year-old brother of the dead child, upon viewing the body, asked, "If Jesus took James to heaven, why didn't he take all of him?" I'm afraid all of us were stunned by the question. I stumbled through a tearful answer.

Because of that experience I have asked myself, what is life?

LIFE BEGINS WITH GOD

In Genesis we read, "God breathed into man and he became a living soul." Taken at face value, that says the breath of God is life. To stop breathing is to die—to be separated from the life of the body. Life depends on the process of breathing. New life in a person—resurrection life—is having God to breathe again into us. What happens then in this "new birth" experience is like getting a second life. The quality of this living is characterized by our relationship to the life giver. My existence has more meaning when I acknowledge its source. A poster I like says "Peace is seeing a sunset and knowing whom to thank."

The point where life is transformed from "deadness" to "aliveness" is when a man recognizes his master. This poem expresses that experience well:

I MET THE MASTER

"I had walked life's way with an easy tread,
Had followed where comforts and pleasure led,
Until one day in a quiet place
I met the Master face to face.

With station and rank and wealth for my goal,
Much thought for my body but none for my soul,
I had entered to win in life's mad race,
When I met the Master face to face.

I met Him and knew Him and blushed to see
That His eyes of sorrow were fixed on me,
And I faltered and fell at His feet that day,
While my castles melted and vanished away.

Melted and vanished, and in their place,
Naught else did I see but the Master's face;
And I cried aloud, 'Oh, make me meek
To follow the steps of Thy wounded feet.'

My thought is now for the souls of men;
I have lost my life to find it again,
E'er since one day in a quiet place
I met the Master face to face."

In summary, the Psalmist says, "He lifted me *up* . . . and set my feet on a firm path, steadying me as I walked, and making me sing."

I do not believe the "up" life can begin without God. These principles, used effectively, will improve all human interaction. To make the most sense, however, God must be at the center of it all. It is this faith that is the foundation on which all self-worth is built. When faith is present, being "up" is a living goal, not just a future hope.

14

Five Assets For the New Life

"In our era, the road to holiness necessarily passes through the world of action."

—Dag Hammarskjold

The ability to cope with the challenges of life is discovered in the arena of developing resources within myself. How I am able to tap my own resources, those of others, and the resources of the universe in a continuing way determines my sense of personal worth, my ability to relate to other people, and my capabilities to live freely and fully.

Living the "up" life is what psychologists have called self-actualization. This process is the result of self-knowledge to which is added honesty, congruent activity and respect for the opportunity and experiences of others.

There is a similarity between the early Christians who called themselves ''Followers of the Way'' and people of many Eastern religions who seek the path, the way or a sense of oneness with the universe. That conquest joins all humanity, religious or non-religious. All men want a happier, more satisfying life. The ''answers'' about how one develops that life are many and have varying degrees of validity. The mature and satisfying life—the ''up'' position in the world—is built around five functional assets.

DON'T PLAY IT SAFE

First is the capability to take a *risk* when others play it safe. Maturity is not to be equated with conservatism or rigidity. Those persons who experience the world as vibrant ''living'' systems of interaction do so through a mixture of pain and pleasure that results from taking risks. That blend causes changes within us. Two forces alternate: the tolerance for pain when I ''hurt'' and the desire for growth--improvement when I am ''secure.'' People become depressed, anxious, negative and lonely when they are *afraid* of failure. The resultant safety produces a lethargic state—safe but inactive. People who by contrast are positive about themselves, eager to engage others, and feel basic acceptance in the world around them face the possibility of failure as normal but not fatal. Learning to know oneself presupposes that I will know *both* my joys *and* my sorrows more thoroughly.

STAND ALONE WHEN NECESSARY

The second functional force of the ''up life'' is the

capability to cope with the *pressure* of personal choices when they differ from those of others, even the majority. Maturity is the willingness to face the hard choices of life; immaturity avoids those decisions. The core of the problem is a lack of integrity. If my response from others dominates my life, I will ultimately become a robot. The placating, non-offensive life stance is emotionally suicidal. The healthy person stands alone when he must. He does not cultivate persecution or force rejection by deliberate obnoxious behavior. However, he puts the maintenance of his integrity before the continuation of popularity.

FULFILL YOUR COMMITMENTS

The capability to *persist* in appropriate commitments when others cease is the third dimension of the "up" life-style. The mature person fulfills his responsibilities to others in the face of personal stress and sacrifice. The immature individual experiences depression because he seeks to escape commitment, to rest without satisfactory work. The "down" man seeks a diversion, a change, a momentary relief; the "up" man can do his understood maximum for today and rest for his new effort tomorrow. The mature man need not fear the judgment of others because he has already honestly evaluated his own actions.

My grandfather regularly said, "A man's word is as good as his bond." That axiom rightly captures some truth. My faith in myself is sustained by my own ability to fulfill commitments to myself and others. The depressed person promises himself he will break a habit or pay his bills on time, but his failure to do so frequently confirms his negative feelings. The "up" man sets realistic goals and disciplines himself to meet them.

BELIEVE IN YOUR SUCCESS

The fourth capability which exhibits the "up" life is accepting one's *success* naturally without feigning undue modesty. The "up" man believes in himself—therefore, he accepts his successes and his failures. He knows the difference between pride and humility. Pride is the inability to accept any self-limits and the pretense that I can accomplish something which is beyond my capabilities. Pride is also the pretense that I cannot do something of which I am capable. It is just as proud (egotistically speaking) to deny the ability to do something as it is to pretend an ability I do not have in order to "save face." Humility is then simply the acknowledgement of what you can honestly do or not do. Pride may often keep a man from attempting a project in which he is afraid he might fail. Real modesty is making the attempt, knowing I run the risk of failure. The "down" life-style is characterized by a false front, a pretense of reality. The "up" life-style enjoys success, gives thanks for good things, and takes each new challenge in turn.

KEEP YOUR EYES OPEN

The fifth capability present in this "up" life is that of maintaining *perspective* in the face of change. "Down" people are often unpredictable and changeable. Many people feel depressed while they remain "hip." They have shifting views, often dominated by the pressures of pleasing others. The ability to maintain values and be consistent to one's basic views in the face of change is a mark of maturity.

Perspective is a delicate balance between the weight of my own prejudice and the burden of adjusting to the domination of others. When I see clearly, I am not blinded by the clouds of my fear or the fog of someone else's criticisms. As I articulate more precisely my own values, the guidelines from my daily experiences are carefully etched from my painful and pleasurable confrontations. Because I accept the responsibility for clearly seeing the pitfalls, I do not blame others for my stumblings. When I succeed in resisting the manipulation of others' demands or seductions, I am also free to accept the rewards of my actions.

When I tap the continuing resources of life, I commit myself to growth. I have discussed the steps to growth, some of the problems with which we cope, and these five capabilities. We now turn to the results of this growth.

15

Restless Happiness

"Let us do with speed now that which will profit us for all eternity."

—St. Benedict

Few people will admit that they do not wish to be happy. Our disagreement is over what will make us happy. In the first part of this book we considered the seven steps to personal growth. These ideas were developed out of a study of Jesus' eight statements on happiness, called the "Beatitudes." Look at this paraphrase of what He said.

1. Happy are those who know they need God; for the kingdom of heaven is theirs!
2. Happy are those who have sorrow; for they can accept comfort.

3. Happy are those who clutch; for the whole earth belongs to them.
4. Happy are those who long to be just and good; for they shall be completely satisfied.
5. Happy are those who show mercy; for they will be kindly treated.
6. Happy are those who are utterly sincere; for they shall see God.
7. Happy are those who make peace; they remind others of God.
8. Happy are those who are persecuted because they are good; for they will appreciate honest judgment from God.

—Matthew 5:3-10

The kind of happiness expressed in those concepts might be called *restless*. When my faith in life fits harmoniously into the universe I will be happy. When I am not in tune with my surroundings, discord results. Yet it is unusual to describe happiness as restless. A unique blend is present in these declarations.

NOT RESTLESSNESS ALONE

Restlessness alone is not a goal for living. It may produce much unhappiness. The aimless search for pleasure is restless. My office is frequented by individuals and couples who are restless but not happy. This kind of situational impulsiveness leads to fruitless and painful predicaments. The desire to have too much too soon—"the instant mania" of our age—lacks the appreciation born of patient discipline. Sexual promiscuity is built on an uncommitted restlessness in the quest for physical satisfaction. This dissatisfied and changeable quality of living is a symptom we generally associate with unhappiness.

On the other hand, happiness links itself mentally to more positive images in our experience. A satisfaction of sorts can be conjured up when one simply thinks the word *happy*. Associations of pleasantness surround the concept of happiness. But how does one *keep* happy? The maintenance of the happy state is a quest for many.

Some people in our society are told to be happy with resting. We "retire" them to the life of leisure. But too often this merely produces a state of unhappy ease. A breed of gray-haired liberationists is on the social horizon, and I champion their cause. Human happiness is quite often built on the sense of purpose or meaning one feels in life. The victories of the past are to be cherished, but they do not satisfy the present urge to be significantly involved. It is an obscene suggestion to a healthy and productive person that he simply stop functioning as a part of his normal cycle.

Many of us are like Billy, the Bible salesman, in "No, No, Nanette" who sang: "I want to be happy, but I won't be happy until I make somebody else happy too." A need to be needed reflects normalcy. The flower of happiness is rarely cultivated in the garden of isolation. Happiness is the warmth of another's response and the planting of seeds that bloom into smiles on the faces of our friends.

Restless happiness is characterized by those succinct words of Robert Browning: "A man's reach should exceed his grasp; or what's a heaven for?" Consider these three aspects of the *happily restless* life.

ANOTHER KINGDOM

First, my restlessness and my happinesss both ultimately belong to another world. A commitment one makes to Christian living is not a non-patriotic one; but the kingdom of our loyalty is eternal. To live with an eternal perspective does not mean escapism. I need not avoid the nasty here and now by hoping for the "sweet by and by." Nor do I want my life to be so heavenly minded that it is no earthly good! A man of faith is a man happy with his life in this world, but aware that a better world is yet to come. Death is an enemy, but not an all powerful one. Since Christ lives beyond the grave, I believe I shall know that same life—the resurrection existence! I am restless for the fulfillment of my ESP—Eternal Stimulated Perspective.

A FULFILLING CHALLENGE

Second, restless happiness is the result of a call to meaningful service. I am on a mission, proud of my position, but aware of its responsibilities. To live the "up" life is the happiness of purpose. Good mental health is stimulated by a sense of belonging and a fulfilling direction for life.

When Jesus announced the official beginning of his service as a public teacher, he read from the Prophet Isaiah these words:

> *The Spirit of the Lord is upon me; He has appointed me to preach Good News to the poor; He has sent me to heal the broken hearted and to announce that captives shall be released and the blind shall see, that the*

> *down-trodden shall be freed from their oppressors and God is ready to give blessings to all who come to Him.*
>
> —*Luke 4:18-19, Living Bible*

Any of those six life assignments—to tell good news, to heal the broken hearted, to pardon prisoners, to heal blind eyes, to set captives free, and to announce God's free blessings—would fill a life with work. The giving of a total life—His life—fulfilled those goals. Nothing short of a life given to others is demanded by those who profess to follow Him.

A FUTURE HOPE

The third dimension of restless happiness is anticipation. The fulfillment of the kingdom of God is like the end of an engagement. The bride has received her ring, the groom has made plans for the honeymoon, but the wedding is just a little way off. Happiness is the mood, but the anticipation of a full marriage adds a restless note to the music of engagement. That note of expectancy does not mean that reality is postponed. To be a Christian is to be people-oriented. The needs of human beings will not be solved by denials. Nor are there problems too devastating to tackle. To be aware of the promise of fulfillment is to be called to new dedication. This perception of life will not necessarily be despised by enemies or praised by friends. Its reality may only be confirmed within the individual spirit. The promise of a special welcome from one who loves us is enough.

During the presidential tenure of Theodore Roosevelt, the chief executive took a safari to Africa to hunt big game. On the same boat returning to the United States was a missionary retiring after 40 years of service in a jungle village. As the boat docked at the harbor, cheering throngs greeted the president on his return. No one was there to meet the missionary. A sudden anger welled within him when he compared 40 years of service to 40 days on a safari. An African student coming to America for study got off the boat with him. The self-pity in the missionary spilled over because no one had come to welcome him home. But his young friend put things in a different perspective when he asked, "Teacher, will there not be a different welcome when we get to our *real* home in heaven?"

One cannot be fully satisfied while yet anticipating a concluding moment. While life can be full and rewarding, we remain restless until we are truly home. Restless happiness is not postponement for the future; it is involvement with further anticipation.

16

What Makes Life Christian?

"When men are animated by the charity of Christ, they feel united, and the needs, sufferings and joys of others are felt as their own."

—Pope John XXIII

Not all that is written or spoken under the banner of "Christian" is acceptable to me. I can declare my distinctions from those who practice a different style of psychological counseling and I can also delineate some differences in my theological perspectives. It is important to define what one means by the word Christian.

I see five essential ingredients in the life and ministry of Jesus that must be embodied in those that claim to follow Him. They are integrity, inspiration, imperative, insight, and immortality. Let me spell them out more fully.

INTEGRITY

The United States in the '70's was shaken by two particular events: the reaction to the Vietnam War and the Watergate incidents. While traveling abroad during those years, I was aware of the sense of uncertainty among countries strongly allied with the free world. They wondered if they could continue to depend on the promises of the United States. For me these events symbolized a loss of national integrity, one which hopefully will not be irreparable. No one planned these events to reflect on our country, but they go into history as black marks on our character as a nation.

Personal integrity can also be lost subtly. It happens so easily, like a boat loosed from its moorings, drifting gently and then more swiftly before it is dashed against the rocks, helpless without a captain to guide it to safety. An essential of the Christian life is to emulate the integrity embodied in the Master. He called himself truth; history records the impact of that truth.

Personal integrity is the living expression of my theology. My integrity is the reflective mirror of my soul. To know truth is to be made free to express the intention of the creator. I will be "believable" only as I live what I say. Consistency between my words and my actions is far more persuasive than the rationality and impressiveness of my creeds. Congruency of action brings believability to my words.

In "My Fair Lady," Eliza Doolittle sings her frustration with words in the lines, "Don't talk of love; show me." The tests of one's experience at the burning bush comes in the fire of confrontation with Pharoah. When I live my faith, I look like a Christian!

INSPIRATION

That's the second ingredient in the recipe of Christian experience—inspiration! For twenty centuries Jesus has turned men's lives around when they encountered Him. He expects no less of me. I am to be an inspiration. These are Jesus' words: "Follow me and I will make you catch men instead of fish." Two of the descriptions given His followers are salt and light. Your life is to add flavor to the lives of others and to eliminate their darkness. Salt changes things and so does light. "Let your light shine that others, seeing your good works, will glorify God, your Father," said Jesus.

Inspiration is a quality, not a commodity. It is not a substitute for integrity; it is the overflow of that fullness from within us. A Christian lives enthusiastically. And that's communicably contagious. To be so refreshing to be around that others are drawn to you is a testament to the "saltiness" of your life. To be marked as an illuminator says I am "lighting my corner" of the world.

Parents and other teachers learn by their children's actions that most of their lessons are absorbed from watching others rather than listening. I "model" my lessons; they are "caught" before they are taught. Perhaps that accounts for the name given Jesus' eight statements about happy living, the BE-atitudes. People would rather *see* a Christian than hear one.

IMPERATIVE

Jesus' invitation to those who first followed Him has been paraphrased like this: "Men, if you follow me, you will be underpaid, with little promise of future financial security. You will be constantly in trouble, but you will be on a significant mission and you will be mysteriously happy." Few applicants would line up for that job! To be a Christian is to enter a life of discipline; His first followers were called disciples. But do not confuse discipline with asceticism or isolation. The imperative is loving behavior. The lawgivers are necessary, but the love givers fulfill the demanding tasks.

The positive "up life" is one based on insistent expectations. The quest will exceed the accomplishment. My imperative is to run the race of life like a winner. When I embody that demand, I focus on my own mission. My time is too valuable in the exercises of living the full life to be embroiled in excuses, blaming others for my behavior, or failing to accept my assignments. Like a great athlete I run against the measure of my best, not against the competition.

The imperative to love is comprehensive. I am to love God unreservedly and to love others as I love myself. Nothing I do is unimportant—worship, work, conversation, leisure, and every other relationship. William Carey summed up the imperative: "Expect great things from God; attempt great things for God."

INSIGHT

The fourth mark of the Christian life is insight—the

ability to see in clear perspective. If the integrity, inspiration, and imperative aspects are burdens, this dimension is an assurance. Listen to the words of Jesus:

> *Don't worry about things—food, drink and clothes. For you already have life and a body—and they are far more important than what to eat and wear. Look at the birds! They don't worry about what to eat—your heavenly Father feeds them. And you are far more valuable to Him than they are. Will all your worries add a single moment to your life?*
>
> —*Matthew 6:25-27,*
> *The Living Bible*

The reality of God's regard for us calms the anxiety of our spirits. Much of our psychological insight is an application of theological truth to life. In my office reception area is a plaque reading: "Never let tomorrow use up today." Worry, fear, and anxiety waste our energies. My limits can cause me to doubt my capability to cope with life. However, when I take only one problem at a time, I discover myself coping effectively. What I cannot handle today, I leave for tomorrow. I give today's effort and tomorrow's concern to my Father, whose love for me is greater than my own.

I love to sing. One of my favorite lyrics I learned as a child is:

> *This is my father's world*
> *And to my listening ears,*
> *All nature sings, and round me rings*
> *The music of the spheres.*

This is my Father's world
I rest me in the thought
Of rocks and trees, of skies and seas,
His hand the wonders wrought.

This is my Father's world
O let me ne'er forget
That though the wrong seems oft so strong
God is the Ruler yet.

This is my Father's world,
The battle is not done.
Jesus who died shall be satisfied
And earth and heaven be one.

—*Maltbie D. Babcock*

To sing those words, or simply read them, reminds me of the ultimate realities. I find it difficult to be down in the face of that truth.

IMMORTALITY

The final ingredient in this personal perspective on Christian living is immortality. My faith is that life never ends. Here is the quantum leap of hope between the followers of Christ and all other religions—the resurrection.

Deep within all of us is a fear that life will be lived; and when it concludes in the grave, there is nothing else. Death is seen as the final punctuation point to life. The transforming mark of the Christian is that I not only believe there is life after death, I also believe that that life makes my existence on earth more meaningful.

If there is no resurrection, the Christian will have been fooled. If there is a resurrection, he will be prepared. To believe in a life after death, however, is to make this life more hopeful. I can bear the pain of separation from those I love because of the hope of reunion beyond the grave.

When I was in graduate school I examined and re-examined my beliefs. I have not given up the process, but it happens much more subtly now rather than rationally or philosophically. One professor of religion was an extremely bright and persuasive man. He did not believe in the resurrection of Christ. I admired his ability to think and to articulate what seemed like a rational position. One day I sought him out for a private conversation. I asked him, "If I give up the resurrection as a part of my faith, what do I put in its place?" I remember the silence that seemed eternal. "Nothing," he said. I admired his honesty, but I felt far less drawn to him.

The next afternoon I had the funeral of a close friend. Driving home alone I pondered the words I had read at his graveside:

> *"I am the resurrection and the life; the man who believes in me, even though he dies like anyone else, shall live again. He is given eternal life and shall never perish."*
>
> *—John 11:25-26*

My professor's "nothing" stood in weak contrast to that strong assurance.

I find the pain of life bearable and its mysteries comprehensible only in the promise of an empty grave!

This immortality transforms my hopelessness into hopefulness. Frederick Nietzch said, "He who has a *why* to live for can bear almost any *how*." The Christian lives in hope—the "up life"—because he believes the day will come when all *whys* will be answered.

CHRISTIAN AND COMPETENT

As a professional my Christian faith is not a substitute for basic skills and training. When a couple comes to my office for marriage counseling, it would be dishonest for me to use that time for evangelism. I believe that a born again Christian should be the finest in his field. Faith becomes a plus to every activity. It is not a crutch on which he leans when he does not know what else to do.

Martin Luther stressed the dignity of each vocation as he led the reformation movement. There are really no unimportant activities in an individual's life, particularly if he sees himself as a Christian. All activity is then dedicated to God. The "clergy" and the "laity" are no longer separate; the barriers are down.

Being up in a down world is having the courage to be who you are. Unfortunately, when other people are also trying to be themselves, conflicts arise. The final section of our consideration in this book will be devoted to the application of this life-style to my relationship with others.

PART FOUR
Personal Experience

"Integrating Your Insights Daily"

''How it improves people for us when we begin to love them.''

—David Grayson

17

People Need People

''We need to have people who mean something to us, people to whom we can turn knowing that being with them is coming home.''

One of the happy discoveries of my life is that people really do need each other. When I first saw the Broadway play ''Funny Girl'' I responded to those words Fanny Brice sang, ''People who need people are the luckiest people in the world.''

Other people are essential to the growing life experience. Psychologists refer to ''the significant others'' in our patterns of interaction. These are the ones who leave their imprint on us as we develop from birth through advanced years.

PARENTS NEED CHILDREN

Parents are obviously the most influential people in our early period. In *Being A Man In A Woman's World* I discussed the impact of the mother upon her child, particularly the male.[6] For boys and girls the possibility of strangling on the emotional umbilical cord is very real. Leah is a good example.

She was brought to counseling by her parents. Her "problem" was rebelliousness. I listened to her mother and father as they described her independence and disobedience. I looked across the room at Leah; she looked 17, but she was actually 25! When I asked her why she was still living at home, she began to talk about how much she *needed* her parents. I came to the conclusion that they needed her. She was being suffocated ("stifled," to use a Bunkerism) in her normal growth by parents who could not let go of "their baby."

UNHEALTHY NEEDS

Unhealthy needs are met in our relationship as well as healthy ones. Because of that I seek to understand my interaction with others. Let me suggest some ways my dependence on others can be unhealthy.

People may be *substitutes*. The obvious situation is the mother who lives *through* her child. She is happy only when the child is; his pain becomes her pain, etc.

Not unlike a mother who lives through her child, a wife may try to live through her husband. Mimi gave herself away when she asked John, "How do *we* vote?" Over their 20 years of married life, she had become so dependent on her husband that only he had opinions. While she professed to be so happy with their lives, she was quite unnecessary! Their marriage was troubled because John was tired of thinking for both of them.

Dependence is a substitution of someone else into my slot of responsibility. Managing that feeling in a healthy way is a major concern of the therapist. In working with couples or individuals, I seek to develop as little dependence as is necessary for the progress of therapy. I may feed my own unhealthy feelings by having people *need* me too much. To need people is healthy; to be overly dependent on them is unhealthy.

When a person is not free to make a decision without first considering another's opinion, he is probably overly dependent. The Personal Orientation Inventory, an instrument used to evaluate one's feelings, calls this dependence "other centeredness." It is the inability to act without the support of others' opinions. Husbands and wives often fall into the trap of being overly dependent in the name of being considerate of each other's feelings. There is a fine line between concern and dependency.

DEPENDENCE AS A DEFENSE

Dependence may also be a mechanism of defense. Introjection is the process of taking into myself the emotions of another. By so doing, I do not have to face the decisions; I simply accept your feelings. If "we" are disappointed, it is your fault. The feelings originated in you, not in me. As an introjector, however, I have no claim of a personal feeling; my feelings all belong to somebody else.

Being overly identified with another person is also an unhealthy substitution.

Mark was a minister who came for help. He enjoyed being the "darling" of his congregation, but he was becoming uncomfortable with the feeling of being their substitutionary "holy man." "Our pastor is such a good man and does so much," he quoted them bitterly. "That seems to relieve the congregation of doing *anything*!" He had so strongly identified himself with *his* people that he had become their expression, a substitute for their struggle with religious realities and service to their own community. The weight of that responsibility was bearing down on him, and he was squirming under the load.

Mark's example reminds us that our own unhealthy needs are often part of the *system* in which we engage in relationships. Here was a congregation that had given up its responsibilities in order to fill the ego needs of their young minister. On the other hand, he realized that he had been seduced by his own need for power and now had too much responsibility to carry. He simply could not do everything. Their system of interaction had initially worked, but the price they would have to pay to continue it was too great for either Mark or the congregation.

A SYSTEM BALANCES

Usually systems function with some kind of balance. Alcoholics drink so that their spouses may nag; spouses nag so that the alcoholics may drink. Each plays a part in balancing the system. They are people who need each other but in negative and destructive patterns.

As a counselor I regularly see families with ''sick'' systems. Sharon was the ''black sheep'' of the family. Most of the conflicts seemed to be between her and another member of the family which consisted of two other sisters and her parents. They had the uncanny ability of manufacturing an argument over almost any subject. It had become such a habit to be in destructive conflict that I assigned them a minimum of two hours a day of open arguments. This is the same methodology one often uses to help an individual break a habit such as smoking. You encourage the person to over-indulge so that he will become tired of his habit. As we worked together, each of the members of the family began to gain some insight about the unspoken ''rules'' of the family. Sharon was the system wrecker. That made her the ''patient'' when the family came for help. But she was not mentally ill. The family needed each other, but in an unhealthy way. Their pattern of interaction was the ''illness.'' When people need each other to fulfill balance in an unhealthy system, someone gets hurt emotionally.

PEOPLE ARE NOT SCAPEGOATS

Another unhealthy way people need others is called *scapegoating*. The connotation of that word—scapegoat—means finding someone else to blame. When I project my negative needs onto you and become critical of you, you have become my scapegoat. People who excuse themselves by blaming others do this. The faultfinder who is socially critical usually reflects his own sense of inadequacy. The only way he can handle his fear of failure is by dumping it on another person. Projection is his psychological mechanism of defense against his inner feelings of weakness.

Parenthetically, the "scapegoat" comes from the Hebrew tradition. When the people of Israel were nomads, the priest symbolized their forgiveness by placing their hands on a goat to transfer the sins of the people into its body. The goat was then banished from the camp to signify the removal of the guilt of the people. We, as the Israelites did, need symbols to express our feelings, but "scapegoating" with other *people* is an unhealthy projection of our feelings onto them. No matter how hard I try, I cannot transfer my feelings to another individual and have him take them away.

People also need people in healthy interaction. I depend on other persons primarily through the avenues of self-disclosure and feedback.

SELF-DISCLOSURE

In the process of sharing what I know and how I feel, I more clearly focus on who I am. There is a sense in which I can only know myself as I reveal myself to you. Obviously this will require a willingness to risk letting you know me. Most of us are afraid of others. Yet we need them.

Two fears compound our desire to be known by others.

AFRAID TO BE KNOWN—PRETENSE

The first is the fear of being known at all. Our behavior

is "masked" behind roles which represent what we perceive to be the expectations of others. I am afraid that you will not admire, appreciate or regard me highly if you learn too much about me. My fear of your rejection keeps my barriers up. What I know about me I judge to be negative, and I project that negative response on to you. I end up lonely behind my self-imposed wall, and you are shut out of my life. That is the fear of being known.

LONELINESS—THE FEAR OF NEVER BEING KNOWN

Fortunately, the second fear is the stronger of the two. It is the fear of never being known. When my loneliness becomes painful, I risk dropping the masks that hide me from you. I have already realized that if I succeed in wearing the false face and you reject me, I will never know whether you would accept the "real me." The real me is behind the mask, and I must lower it in order to find out whether or not you will accept me. When I disclose my inner feelings, I need a positive reception. It is not easy to strip away my emotional defenses. Often the cause of initial self-disclosure is a crisis.

Harold was a big man. He towered over me as he entered the office and lowered his massive weight into the chair. He took little time to tell me that he was also a man broken in spirit. His divorce from the woman he loved had just become final. Her parting remark to him had been, "I hope, for your sake, someone can crack that shell. I give up." He began to tell me a familiar story. He was brought up in an emotionally repressive home where he had learned not to express feelings, particularly "weaknesses" like tears. He was rarely touched as a child and did not learn how to reach out to others for comfort. He had learned to be a loner, strong and silent. He didn't *need* anybody . . . or so he thought.

When his third wife left him, he felt like he had been "hit in the head by a two by four stick of lumber." For the first time he could remember he cried . . . and finally wept uncontrollably. Then he thought of suicide. That's when he came to me.

Self-disclosure was a painful thing for Harold. But he learned not only to share with me but also to open up to other people as part of a growth group. He needed others. It was just difficult to admit it.

As I find others receptive and responsive, it becomes easier for me to share myself with them. It is, however, not the responsibility of others to force me into self-disclosure. I am the only one who can control my sharing. No one really has the capacity to know what is within me. To expect others to read my mind or to guess what I feel is ludicrous. If I fail to open up to you, I allow you to *assume* things at my own risk.

FEEDBACK

What I cannot do alone is to see myself. I need you to be my "mirror" in order that through your eyes, ears and senses I may get a reflection of myself. I am blind to my own actions and your reactions without your "feedback." Look back at the descriptions of this process under the "Assessment" step of personal growth in Chapter Six. Your verification of my self-perception is the key ingredient in feedback.

People need people. Interdependence on another in a giving and receiving process is healthy interaction. ''Down'' people are isolated and closed. ''Up'' people recognize their need for others and risk disclosure in order to make contact.

Up and down are directional signals. In order to know which direction you're traveling, your life compass must distinguish between the two. Maybe you've been heading in the wrong direction. Try losing to win! Sound crazy? Read on.

18

Try Losing!

''All I have seen teaches me to trust in all I have not seen.''

Yes that's the paradox—winners may lose and losers may win. If you have grown up on the diet of competitive athletics, education, social climbing, and generally *winning* that I did, ''losing'' doesn't seem like the way to go ''up.''

Jesus put it this way:

> *''Whoever loses his life for My sake, will save it, but whoever insists on keeping his life will lose it; and what profit is there in gaining the whole world when it means forfeiting one's self?''*
>
> —*Luke 9:24-25, The Living Bible*

Most of us look at life as a process of *getting* and the idea of giving seems foreign. We live in a consuming age—we *use up* things. ''Throw away'' items fill the shelves of our stores. The proliferation of convenience devices adds to our desires for ''quickness.'' We have an ''instant'' mania. Within these advances of improved living, we have discovered some problems. One is an energy crisis. We have found that our demand for natural gas, for instance, will exhaust our supply of resources within a few years. *Getting* has produced a problem. It is extremely disappointing to have a room full of electric appliances and not have any power to generate them; or to have numerous gas-driven vehicles and appliances and have no source of energy for them.

A similar emotional powerlessness creates the ''down'' in our lives. We seek to consume personally. But the secret of upmanship is in giving, not taking.

WE KEEP WHAT WE GIVE AWAY

David Dunn wrote a book called *Try Giving Yourself Away*. It tells about what he called his hobby of self-giving. He is a man who has learned that there is more benefit from giving than in receiving.

Among my favorite wall hangings is one on which is engraved the words: ''The only love we keep is the love we give away.'' When I am tempted to withhold myself from another, I am often reminded of that message.

Being *up* in a *down* world is first a matter of perception of direction. I need to know the way up. It is easy to miscalculate that direction in our society. The *top* so often seems to be a higher salary, a bigger home, greater social recognition, and a collection of things to show the measure of my worth. Sometimes the crises or tragedies of life befriend us with a jolt back into reality.

Ken was on his way up. He had worked hard and learned all of the tricks for outsmarting competitors. He was going to be a success. He was not quite sure what that meant, but he pursued his ever increasing quotas and never failed once to be the "number one salesman" for his company. He had gained almost everything money could buy, but he was depressed. "How do I get out of this rat race?" he asked me. My reply was, "Try losing!"

You cannot win all the prizes in life without losing something else. The choice is an inevitable one. Ken chose to put his values in priority. His 12-year-old son beamed when his father came to a basketball game. He was an all-star in his league, and his dad had never seen him play. Ken and his wife took a weekend retreat with some other couples to enrich their marriage. His wife confessed that she never really expected the weekend to materialize because she anticipated a cancellation in favor of a sales conference. He began losing some contracts to others who seemed to be on the way up in the industry. Ken appeared to be on a standstill or even a down grade. Yet he was happier than he had been in years. "There are some things that money can't buy and success can't bring you," Ken said to me. "I know what I feel, but I can't put a price tag on it." When our priorities get turned in the right direction our feelings usually follow.

CHANGE IS WORTH IT

Have you ever picked up a dried cocoon from the

ground or off a tree limb? The empty, lifeless shell was once the home of a butterfly. Before that it was a slimy caterpillar. In the process of change a beautiful butterfly emerged.

I was recently speaking at a conference for women in Florida, and Kathy introduced me to a book called *Hope for the Flowers* by Vicki Paulas. The story told there is worth sharing.

Stripe was a young caterpillar who had discovered he could crawl. In his adventures he came to a mass of caterpillars, each climbing over the other trying to get to the top of the "caterpillar pillar." With zest he began climbing too, hoping to discover what was at the top. None of the other climbers seemed to have the time to answer his questions about why everyone was climbing. In the course of his climb he met Yellow, obviously a female. They both continued their struggle toward the top, but as they became acquainted, they decided to leave the pile of caterpillars and just be with each other. They did, but Stripe was still curious about the top of the pillar. While he was returning to the climb, Yellow became a butterfly.

The story continues with Yellow's attempts to communicate with Stripe while he discovers that there is nothing at the top of the pillar. It is a captivating analogy of life.

THE REAL GIFT

Ralph Waldo Emerson once wrote: "Rings and jewels are not gifts, but apologies for gifts. The only gift is a portion of thyself." Giving yourself is in contrast to the demanding, consuming tone that pervades our modern era. We are getters, climbers who are seeking the unknown at the top of the heap. We believe that the direction of happiness is "above" others. Yet we discover that it is in the act of putting "down" our barriers and reaching out to others that we are able to become human. Caterpillars don't fly; butterflies fly. But in order to fly they must give up their crawling shells. That is true with humans too.

What *lasts* is generated from within us; it cannot be measured by all the possessions external to one's spirit. I gain only by giving away. I keep those gifts of the spirit—parts of myself—that I lose to others. The act of giving a part of one's being is eternal. Things I give you may grow old or be consumed, but you may retain a part of me within you forever. That is the secret of giving. I first gain because of the joy I get from giving myself to you. My second benefit is the pleasure I see in you through receiving my gift. I often may receive a third positive result, the spontaneous reaction in which you give a portion of yourself back to me.

You do not have to be rich to be generous. You need to learn only one lesson: Giving beats getting. Start with what you have—yourself. You are the only valuable item which you can give away and yet never really lose. Try losing—in the paradox of giving, it is the only way to win.

19

Don't Misspell Life!

"I hear and I forget;
I see and I remember;
I write and I understand."
—A Chinese Proverb

Being alive in a deadening surrounding is a matter of perspective. We often see only what we want to see. One interesting method for evaluating your view of life is to see if you misspell the word by the manner of your living.

DECEPTION: THE "LIE" PLAN

If you observe the life-style of some persons, there appear to be only three letters in the word "life": they are LI E! With the "F" omitted, the word changes. Living is not really ''lie-ing.'' Yet sometimes it seems easier to travel by pretence than by truth. One of the emotional symptoms of down living is its falseness.

''Phony role playing'' is a prime characteristic of deceptive living. When I manipulate you I deceive not only you but myself by denying that there is any other potential value for our relationship. That denial produces deadness in my emotional centers. I cannot risk failure or ''losing'' by giving of myself; so I revert to all the mechanisms which help me control you. I must treat you like an object and ''master'' our encounters before you can discover my tricks and embarrass me. I manipulate you in so many different ways that often those very actions on my part begin to control me. I must use all my energies to concentrate on my own survival.

Sir Walter Scott wrote, ''Oh, what a tangled web we weave, when first we practice to deceive!'' To spell life as a lie, a delusion of others, is also to be self-deceived. The words a woman alcoholic said to me can best sum up the results: ''I've lied to so many people about so many things, I don't even know what the truth is anymore.'' Her style of living turned life into a lie. When I live under a pretense, I can only spell life with three letters.

CONDITION: THE ''IF'' PLAN

When you observe the way some other people live, the word life seems to contain only two letters—''if.'' The focus of most life energies in this system is toward rationalizing situations. The ''if'' plan is a style to explain all failures. My mistakes are seen in the light of improper conditions. "If this had happened, then . . ." becomes a standard explanation. I rationalize all errors. I take little responsibility without an excuse for my ineffectiveness. I become clever at placing blame on others rather than accepting the results of my own behavior. Eric Berne described this behavior in his book *Games People Play* under the heading "If it weren't for you." Conditional rationalization is described in that game.

Postponement for the future is another expression of the conditional life-style. Tomorrow is another way of saying "if." Martin Van Bee said, "Today is the tomorrow we worried about yesterday." Living by the method of procrastination is not patience; it is deadening to action. Whatever can be done today is all that is likely to be done. Otherwise I may end up like the tragic man described in this bit of verse:

He was going to be all that he wanted to
be—tomorrow.
None would be braver or kinder than
he—tomorrow.
A friend who is troubled and weary he knew,
On him he would call and see what he could
do—tomorrow.
Each morning he stacked up the letters he'd write
And thought of the folks he would fill with
delight—tomorrow.
The greatest of workers this man would have
been—tomorrow.
The world would have hailed him had he ever
seen tomorrow.
But, in fact, he passed on, he faded from view,

And all that he left when living was through
Was a mountain of things that he intended to
do—tomorrow.

ISOLATION: THE "I" PLAN

The most limited view of life is the self-centered one. When I can see no one but myself and live only for my interest, the perimeters of my world shrink. Ben Franklin is credited with saying, "The smallest package in the world is a man wrapped up in himself."

There is a difference in self-assertiveness and isolation. Many people have to be taught to use the word *I* in order to gain self-identity and to feel good about positive steps toward personal responsibility. The isolated man is interested only in the "getting" life. He does not share interaction; he dominates it. He does not listen; he talks. He has no time to feel the pain of others; his own discomfort preoccupies his energies. His wishes are predominant over the needs of others; he comes first, and so on ad nauseum.

The life of the isolated man is like the Dead Sea. Even the fresh intake is destroyed by the stale water already present.

INVITATION: THE "FOUR LETTER PLAN"

Upness as a life-style has four capital letters in the word, LIFE! To see living from this perspective is to be invited to total involvement. Emotional aliveness is made up of an orientation to truth, creative expression of myself, the willingness to exercise freedom, and healthy self-assertion. When I spell life with all four letters, it means fully loving, interacting, focusing on others, and enthusiastically engaging the multiple levels of living. I cannot only realistically express myself but I can also enjoy reinforcing your growth and sharing our individual and mutual experiences. It is this whole life, the actualized and fully potentialized life that we seek.

When you read the invitations of Jesus, there is an interesting similarity in them. Look at these:

> *"Anyone who listens to My message and believes in God who sent Me has eternal life . . ."*
>
> —*John 5:24, The Living Bible*

> *"I am the one who raises the dead and gives them life again. Anyone who believes in Me, even though he dies . . . shall live again."*
>
> —*John 11:25, The Living Bible*

> *"I am the Way—yes, and the Truth, and the Life. No one can get to the Father except by means of me."*
>
> —*John 14:6, The Living Bible*

> *"The Scriptures point to me! Yet you won't come to me so that I can give you this eternal life."*
>
> —*John 6:40*

All of these statements lead to the word *life*. He saw himself as a source of living, and he invited others to share his life.

When we are truly living the actualized, fulfilled life, we become vibrant, enthusiastic invitations to other persons to discover their own wholeness. The "up" person is contagious; he can infect others with a seed germ that flowers into an appetite for self-discovery and personal growth.

Knowing how to spell life with all four letters is being "up" in a "down" world.

20

Sign On The Dotted Line

"The creation of a thousand forests is in a single acorn."

"How do I begin this personal growth?" Wanda asked me. "I'm tired of the way I've been living. I want to change." Perhaps you feel like she did. Let me close this book with some very basic applications of the philosophical, psychological, and theological insights we have explored together.

I am persuaded that almost every person can change his life. You do not have to live in a down world—depressed, anxious, feeling worthless and lonely. What I have shared with you is largely my experiences in personal growth and in professional counseling. If you will try out these concepts, they will work for you. If you need further help, go to a qualified professional.[7]

The place to begin is to decide you want your life to be different. Say aloud to yourself that you are ready to change; you need to hear that commitment from your own lips. Next open your life to the presence of God. The terms you use are unimportant. Call it meditation, confession of your sins, prayer, praising God—all of these express your openness to His spirit. (By the way, God is not limited to houses of worship. Your home, office, car, an airplane, or a motel room can be a "sanctuary" for this experience.) God is ready when you are.

The next step is to tell another person close to you about your decision to change. You may choose a good friend, a parent, your husband or wife; anyone who cares about you and will be interested in this decision will be suitable. Tell them that you not only are ready to change, but that you need some help from them in the process.

Take a sheet of paper or a pad for the next step. Write these three sentences at the top of three different pages:

1. Today I am going to be *honest* with someone. I am tired of pretending to be something I am not.
2. Today I will be *hopeful*. I am weary of pessimism; I will expect a *good* experience in my life.
3. Today I want to be *helpful* to someone. I will try giving a part of myself to another person.

During the next week, write down as many brief

descriptions of your experiences as you can. When you fill the original sheets, begin new ones. (You will find some space at the back of this book designed for your notes as well.)

One new experience a day written on each sheet will be a *good* start. These are some examples others have shared with me from their ''honesty'' sheets:

> ''I finally told my mother that her advice-giving irritated me. I asked her for some room to grow.'' (Female, age 29)
>
> ''I talked to my boss today about a more challenging job. He listened and was encouraging. Wow!'' (Male, age 32)
>
> ''I admitted to my math teacher I was lost in her class. She offered to help me after school. I couldn't believe it.'' (Male, age 15)
>
> ''I told my wife I feel inadequate as a lover. We agreed to get help together.'' (Male, age 42)

Here are some shared statements from ''hopefulness'' sheets.

> ''I have been afraid to drive on the freeway. Today I tried. I am going back tomorrow.'' (Female, age 50)
>
> ''I told my boy he had a good report card and I was *proud* of him. He smiled big. I liked that too.'' (Male, 36)
>
> ''I applied for a job today. The lady was real nice. I may get it.'' (Female, 17)

> "I tried to be up today and act positively. I made two sales before noon." (Male, 25)

Here are the descriptions of four "giveaway" experiences from typical "helpful" sheets.

> "Last week I wrote a letter to a friend to thank her for encouraging me. She wrote back right away. I feel much closer to her now, like she is a better friend." (Femalc, 22)
>
> "I thanked my minister for his good sermon. I think I saw a tear in his eye. Maybe he needs me too." (Male, 44)
>
> "I tried helping my dad clean the yard. He didn't yell at me all day." (Male, 12)
>
> "You won't believe this. I washed the dishes and cleaned the kitchen last night. My old lady was tickled pink." (Male, 28)

None of these examples is cited because it should be a guideline for your behavior. Real people saw these happenings as their first step to a better way of life. Your first steps may look quite different, but they need not be anymore dramatic than these examples.

After you have tried this initial phase, look back and evaluate what has been different in your life. Make up some goals for yourself for the second week.

Being "up" in a "down" world begins with today. May you discover a lift from the mire of yesterday's discouragement and hope for tomorrow's new opportunity. Sign here. Change begins in that process.

I want to begin today to live the ''up'' life!

Signed

....

The Beginning

HONESTY—Today I am going to be honest with someone. I am tired of pretending to be something I am not.

HOPEFULNESS—Today I will be hopeful. I am weary of pessimism; I will expect a *good* experience in my life.

HELPFULNESS—Today I want to be *helpful* to someone. I will try giving a part of myself to another person.

My First Goal

My Second Goal

My Third Goal

FOOTNOTES

1. Sidney Jourard, *The Transparent Self.*

2. (Memorial Day Address, 1884), John Bartlett, *Familiar Quotations*, 13th Edition, Boston: Little, Brown & Company, 1955, p. 708.

3. Hobart Mowrer, *The Crisis in Psychiatry and Religion* and *The New Group Therapy*.

4. For information, write to The International Family Foundation, 204 Northside Medical Center, 275 Carpenter Drive, Atlanta, Georgia 30328.

5. Virginia Satir, *Peoplemakers*.

6. James E. Kilgore, *Being a Man in a Woman's World*, Harvest House Publishers, Irvine, California, 1975.

7. For marriage and family counselors, membership in the American Association of Marriage and Family Counselors is a strong indication of good, professional preparation.